SHAPE LAND

DiAMOND S FiRST DAY OF SCHOOL

By Bint Smith
Illustrated by Aneeza Ashraf

Hi, my name is Diamond, and I turned five years old this past summer on the 10th of July. Monday will be my first day of school. I will be going to Kindergarten. I am so nervous. What if no one likes me? What if everyone is bigger than me? What if I am bigger than everyone and no one wants to be my friend? What if I am not smart enough? Wait what if I can't remember all of my alphabets. Let me see... A B C D E F G H I J K I M O P Q R S T U V Y and Zeeee.

Oh, no wait, I don't know my alphabet, that doesn't sound right.

Mom! Mom! Help me I can't go to school!

"Why baby? You were so excited earlier."
"Yes but … but mom I don't know all of my alphabets."
"Yes, you do baby we have been working on them all summer."
"No mom see... when I say them, they don't sound right. This song doesn't sound right mommy. Listen Mom listen A B C D E F G H I J K I M O P Q R S T U V W Y and Zeeee."

"What about my numbers? What if I don't remember all of them?" Diamond calm down you will do just fine. Come on let's say them. Now you start, and I will help if you need it. Go ahead baby, say them." 1 2 3 4 5 6 7 8 9 10. "Now together with mommy 11 12 13 14 15 16 17 18 19 20."

"Yay I did it!" "Very good baby, now say your alphabets with mommy. A B C D E F G H I J K L M N O P Q R S T U V W X Y and Z now I know my ABC's next time won't you sing with me."

For the rest of the day, I sung my ABC's and 123's, making sure I did not forget them for school tomorrow. I counted everything that night.
At dinner, I counted the peas on my plate.

When it was time for bed, I counted the steps as I walked upstairs

At bath time I tried to count the bubbles, but they just kept popping.

While in the bed I sang my ABC's until I fell asleep. Goodnight ABC's see you to-morrow.

The next day, I went to school and everyone was so nice to me. All of the kids were trying to help me put my things away because I'm a little short. I guess I'm not the tallest after all.

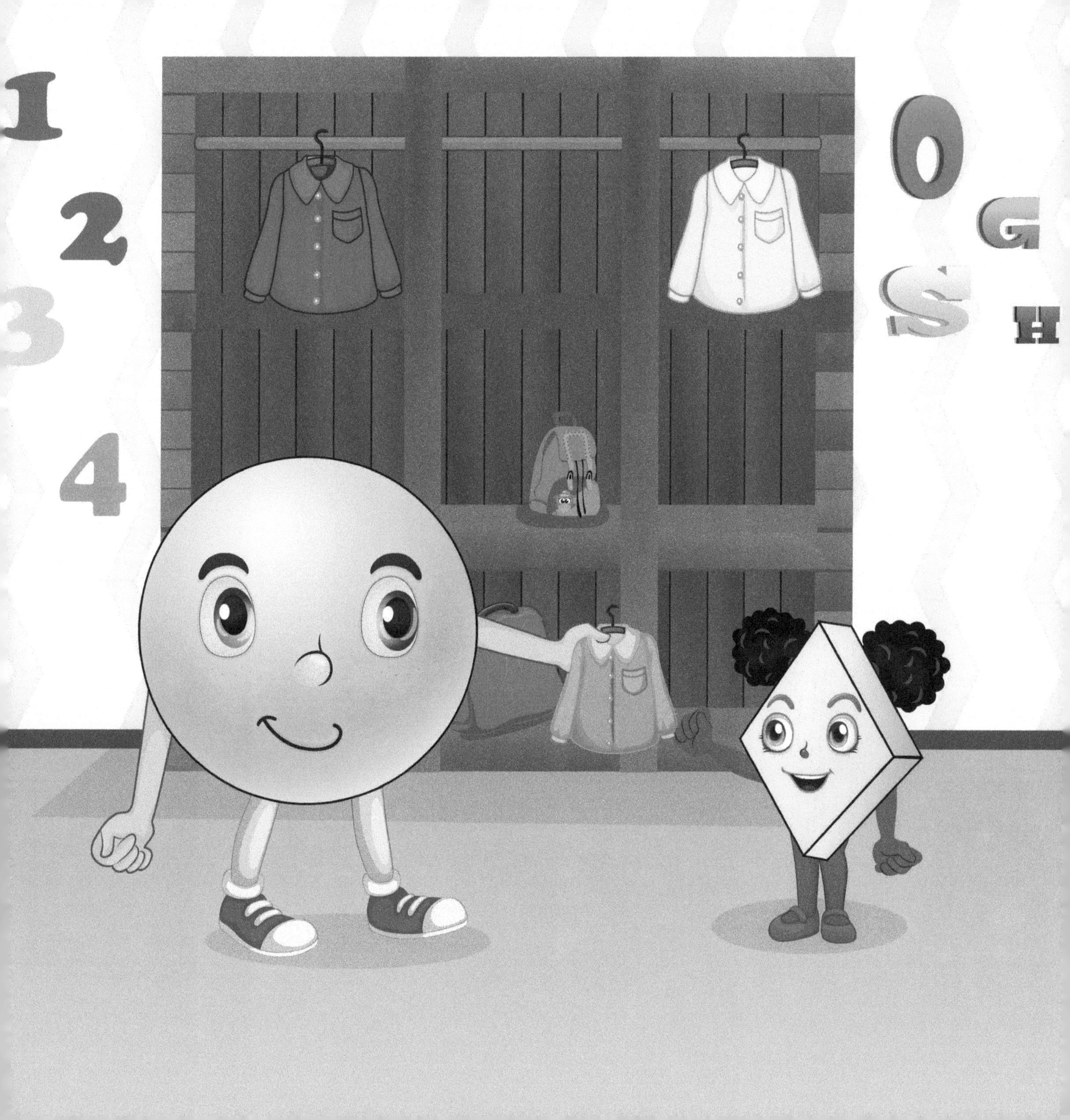
1
2
3
4
O
G
S
H

The teacher said, good morning everyone, have a seat. I am your kindergarten teacher, Miss Square. I sat down on the alphabet carpet for my teacher, so she could begin her lesson. Now who knows their alphabets?

I jumped with excitement and said I do I do. Circle jumped up and said me too Miss Square. That's good, now who can count to twenty? I jumped and yelled out I can! I can! and I started counting really fast 1 2 3 4 5 6 7 8 9 10 11 12 13 14 15 16 17 18 19 20.

That's good! Today we will be working on the letter "A" and the number one. I leaned over to my new friend circle and said this should be easy, I already know this stuff.

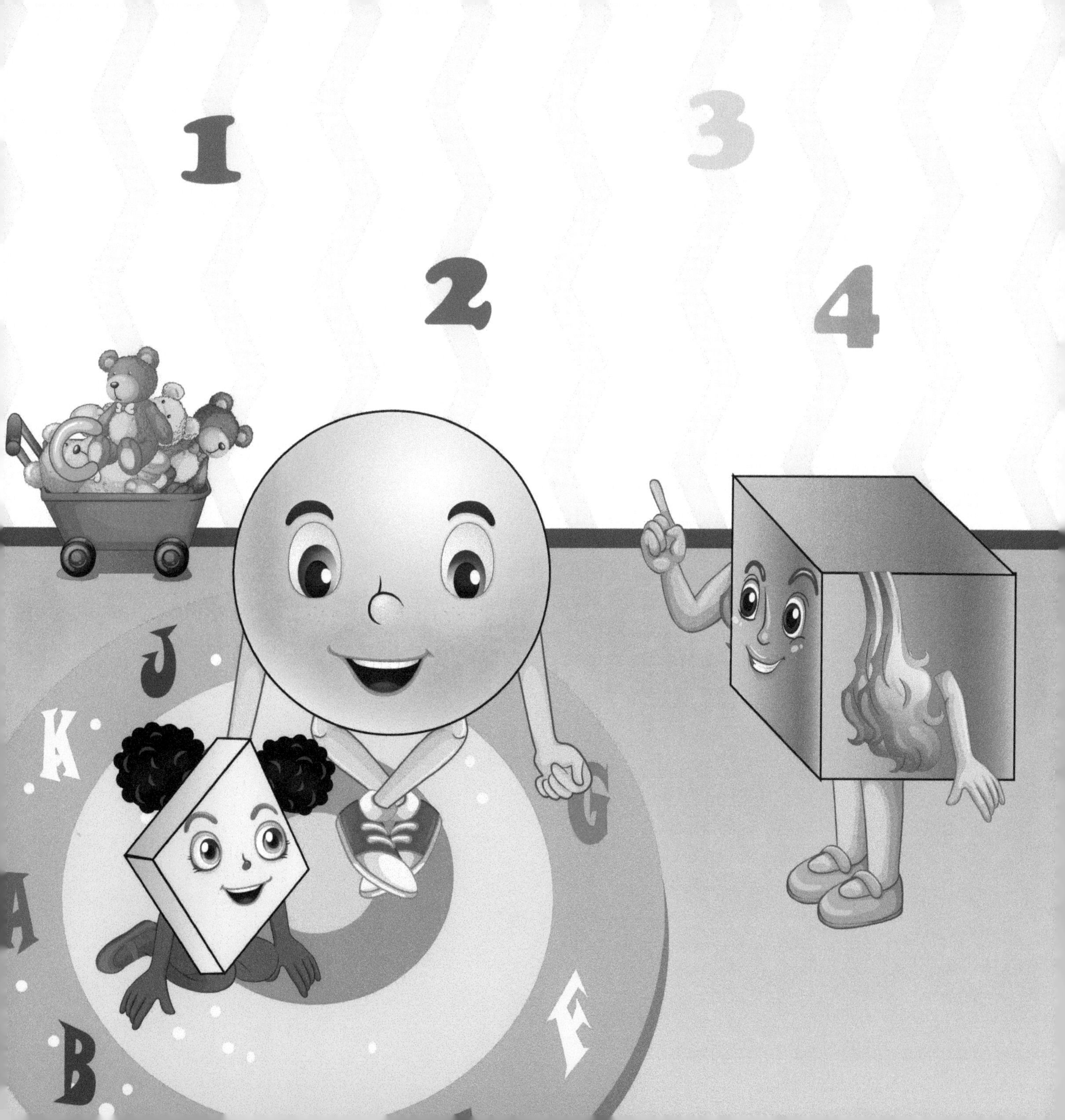

1
2
3
4
J
K
A
B
G
F

Later when my parents came to pick me up from school, I was so happy to tell them about my day. My mom and dad asked, so how was your first day of kindergarten?" "It was so much fun! We colored, we went outside, we played with toys and I made some new friends. My new best friend name is Circle. Then my mom and dad asked so what did you learn today?" "Well, today we learned about the letter "A" and the number one. What's your teachers name, my dad asked. My teacher's name is Miss Square. Then my mom said to me, See, you were all worried about nothing."

The End

The moral of the story is:

We do not know it all, We go to school to learn and become better at whatever it is we do.

Questions you can ask your child/Student at the end of the story.

1. Were you afraid to go to school on your first day?

2. Did you know all your alphabets when you started school?

3. Did you make friends on your first day of school?

CPSIA information can be obtained
at www.ICGtesting.com
Printed in the USA
LVHW020725131220
674007LV00003B/74

9 780578 652986